I0605235

Dealing with
Disorders and Disease

Down Syndrome

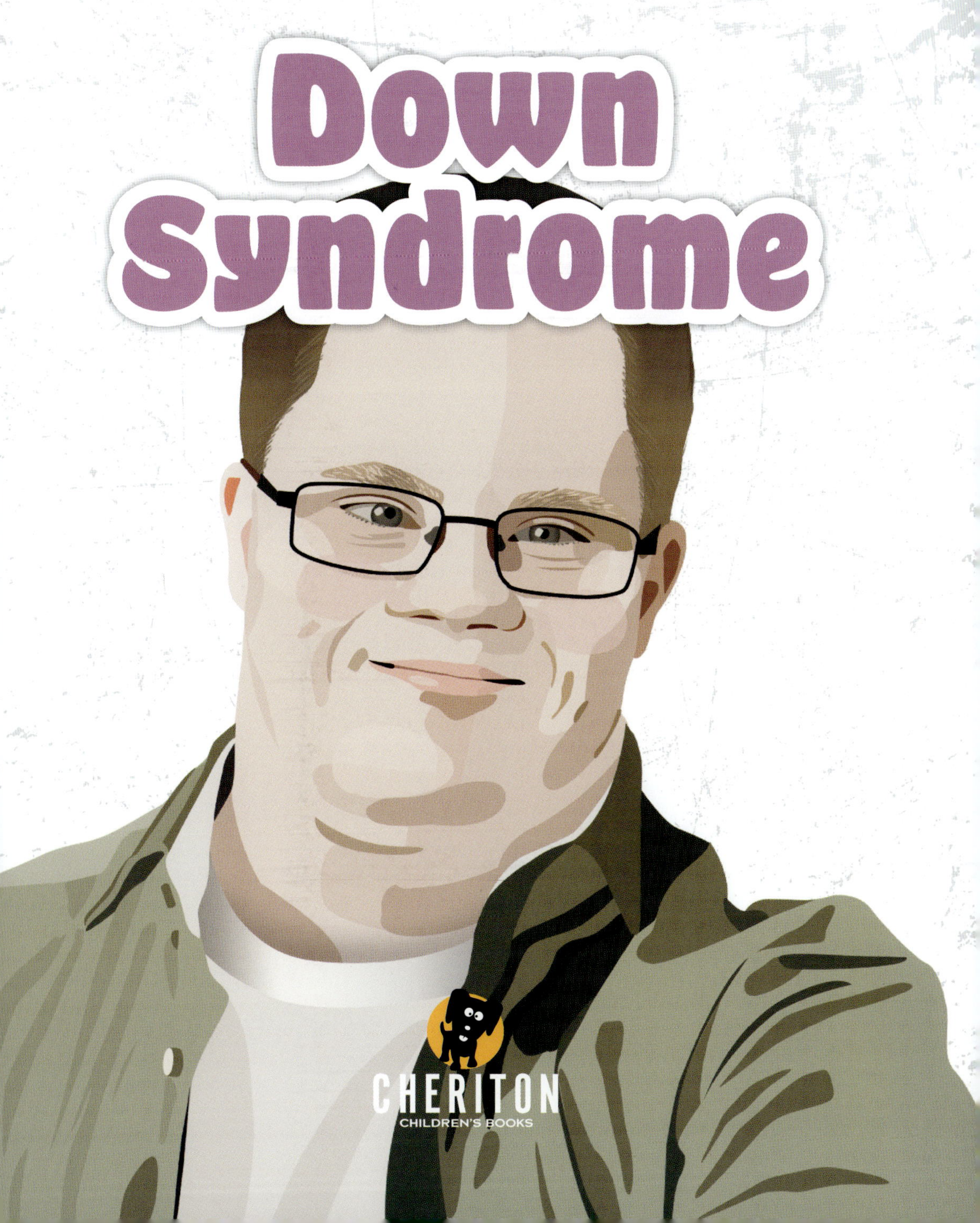

CHERITON
CHILDREN'S BOOKS

Published in 2025 by **Cheriton Children's Books**
1 Bank Drive West, Shrewsbury, Shropshire, SY3 9DJ

First Edition

Author: Sarah Eason
Designer: Paul Myerscough
Editor: Jennifer Sanderson
Proofreader: Ellie James

Picture credits: Cover illustration by Doodle Press. Inside: p4: Shutterstock/SeventyFour, p6: Shutterstock/Eleonora Os, p7: Shutterstock/LightField Studios, p8: Shutterstock/LightField Studios, p9: Shutterstock/Krakenimages.com, p11: Shutterstock/Mangkorn Danggura, p12: Shutterstock/Ground Picture, p14: Shutterstock/Billion Photos, p16: Shutterstock/Nixx Photography, p17: Shutterstock/Kateryna Kon, p18: Shutterstock/Dee-sign, p19: Shutterstock/Chanintorn V, p21: Shutterstock/Karelnoppe, p22: Shutterstock/Sumroeng Chinnapan, p23: Shutterstock/Gorodenkoff, p24: Shutterstock/Elena Pavlovich, p25: Shutterstock/Dimid 86, p26: Shutterstock/Inna Dodor, p27: Shutterstock/Yurchanka Siarhei, p28: Shutterstock/Prostock Studio, p29: Shutterstock/Sirtravelalot, p30: Shutterstock/Southworks, p31: Shutterstock/Denis Kuvaev, p32: Shutterstock/Ground Picture, p35: Shutterstock/Eleonora Os, p36: Shutterstock/Tatiana Diuvbanova, p37: Shutterstock/Monkey Business Images, p38: Shutterstock/Soda O2, p39: Shutterstock/Pixel Shot, p40: Shutterstock/Monkey Business Images, p42: Shutterstock/Ground Picture, p43: Shutterstock/Alexander Raths, p45: Shutterstock/Halfpoint, p47b: Shutterstock/Stock Bird, p47t: Shutterstock/Drazen Zigic, p48: Shutterstock/Krakenimages.com, p50: Shutterstock/LightField Studios, p52: Shutterstock/Monkey Business Images, p53: Shutterstock/Dean Drobot, p54: Shutterstock/Monkey Business Images, p55: Shutterstock/Pressmaster, p56l: Shutterstock/Jacob Lund, p56r: Shutterstock/Halfpoint, p58: Shutterstock/Ground Picture.

Disclaimer: The photographs shown in this book are intended to support the factual content. The publisher notes that the individuals shown in the photographs do not necessarily have the condition/s described in the book.

Printed in China

Contents

CHAPTER 1

Understanding Down Syndrome

Down syndrome is a condition that some children are born with. It is a genetic condition, meaning that it has to do with a difference in a person's genes. This difference in the genes causes certain characteristics associated with Down syndrome. Genes are the parts of a cell that control or influence the way a person looks, grows, and develops.

Naming the Condition

Down syndrome is named for John Langdon Down, an English doctor who was the first person to write a full and accurate description of Down syndrome. The word "syndrome" means "a set of symptoms, or changes, that are caused by a condition." Although Down identified the condition and its symptoms, or signs, he never discovered what caused it. It wasn't until 1959 that French scientist Jerome Lejeune published a paper that explained that Down syndrome is a genetic condition.

The majority of children with Down syndrome usually start to do things such as sitting up, crawling, and walking a little later than other children do.

Physical Signs

Children born with Down syndrome tend to have certain physical features in common. These include a rounded face with eyelids that slope upward slightly, fairly small ears, and a tongue that tends to stick out of the mouth slightly. When they are born, children with Down syndrome are an average size and weight, but they tend to grow a little more slowly than most children. They are usually rather short in height and slightly stockier in build as they grow up. Their muscles tend to be slightly looser and floppier than most people's.

Developmental Difficulties

Down syndrome also affects the way most children learn and develop mentally and emotionally. People with Down syndrome will usually have difficulty learning and remembering the same things as other people, which means that although they can and do develop skills throughout their lives, they will learn to talk, read, and write later than other children usually do. They reach these goals, but at a different pace.

You may know someone with Down syndrome because it is relatively common. In the United States it is the most common chromosomal disorder. A chromosomal disorder is caused by changes in an unborn baby's genes as it develops. Around the world, each year about 3,000 to 5,000 children are born with Down syndrome. In this book, we will look at what causes Down syndrome, how it can be treated, and what it is like to live with this condition.

"Down syndrome is a complex condition that affects people in many different ways."

Health Complications

While many children with Down syndrome lead healthy lives, others have more serious birth defects or medical problems that affect their lives and require extra care and medical attention. Some of the more common health problems among children with Down syndrome involve hearing and vision. In fact, around half of all children with Down syndrome have problems with their eyes and up to 75 percent may suffer some level of hearing loss.

People with Down syndrome often need glasses to help correct problems with vision. Sixty percent of children with the condition will need glasses by the time they go to school.

Problems with Hearing and Vision

Hearing loss can be related to repeated ear infections, fluid buildup in the inner ear, or the way the ears are formed. One common sight problem is strabismus, or being cross-eyed, a condition in which a person's eyes do not properly line up with each other when they look at an object. People with Down syndrome are often nearsighted so things far away appear blurry, or farsighted so things are blurry close-up. They also have an increased risk of eye diseases such as cataracts, which are cloudy areas on the lenses inside the eyes.

Heart Conditions

Almost half of all children born with Down syndrome will have a problem with their heart. Many of these defects, or physical problems, can be quite serious. For example, there is sometimes a small hole or opening in the center of the heart. Some heart problems can even be life-threatening. In these cases, it is important that medical treatment is provided. Some children with Down syndrome are also at an increased risk of developing pulmonary hypertension—a serious condition that can lead to dangerous damage to the lungs. More than half of all people with Down syndrome also suffer from sleep apnea, a condition that causes a person to periodically stop breathing while asleep.

Understanding Down Syndrome

Other less-common health problems that may occur more frequently in children with Down syndrome include digestive system problems, epilepsy, asthma, and an increased risk of infections. There is also a higher risk of anemia, which is a condition in which red blood cells fail to carry enough oxygen to the body; and iron deficiency, which is a type of anemia in which the red blood cells don't have enough iron to be healthy. In infancy or early childhood, some children with Down syndrome get leukemia, a form of blood cancer that can be very dangerous. Fortunately, many of these conditions are treatable.

People with Down syndrome have an increased risk of becoming overweight compared with other children, so maintaining an active lifestyle and eating healthily is very important.

Different People

Around one in three Americans knows someone who has Down syndrome. According to the Centers for Disease Control and Prevention (CDCP), approximately 1 in every 700 babies in the United States is born with Down syndrome, which means about 6,000 babies with Down syndrome are born here each year. Each one of those babies is different and unique.

All Individuals

There are some similarities between people who have Down syndrome, but there is also a huge range of differences. Everyone who has Down syndrome is an individual and is different from everyone else in the way they look, their personality, and the things they can do. They may have no health problems, or a range of different health problems.

A Wide Range of Interests

Just like people without a disability, people with Down syndrome may enjoy very different interests. They may love being creative, have a lot of artistic talent, and excel in drawing, painting, crafting, or music. Other people with Down syndrome love physical activities, and take part in many sports programs and outdoor activities. People with Down syndrome often enjoy communicating with others. They may be great storytellers and public speakers. Others are talented with technology such as computers, tablets, or smartphones. They often develop strong skills in gaming and social media.

People with Down syndrome may have some or many learning disabilities, but, just like most people, they will also have a lot of different interests and abilities.

Understanding Down Syndrome

At present, there is no cure for Down syndrome, but there are many support and educational programs that can help children and adults with the condition, as well as their families. There's no way to tell at birth what a child with Down syndrome will be capable of as they grow up. But most children who are born with this condition get the extra help they need to learn to read and write, and they gain other skills throughout their lives.

With the right treatments and skills, people with Down syndrome can get a job when they grow up so they can earn their own living and care for themselves.

Education and Down Syndrome

As children with Down syndrome grow up, many learn to speak, write, and read just like other children. However, having learning difficulties simply means they need to learn in different ways from other people, and it may take them a little longer to learn new things. Children with Down syndrome may require additional time, repetition of instructions, and extra help to grasp new ideas and skills as part of their education.

PHYSICAL BARRIERS TO LEARNING

Children and young people with Down syndrome often experience delays in fine motor skills, such as being able to hold a pen or pencil to write and draw or cutting with a pair of scissors. That can affect their ability to write and take part in art classes. They may also have difficulties with gross motor skills, which include balance, coordination, and movement. That can have an impact on their ability to take part in physical activities such as sports and their ability to navigate a school or college campus.

MENTAL BARRIERS TO LEARNING

Problems with attention and concentration are also an issue in students with Down syndrome. That can make it difficult for them to focus on a task and join in with learning activities that require a longer time span. People with Down syndrome may often have difficulties with memory and organization, which can affect their ability to retain information, follow directions, and then apply what they have learned in new situations. Because many children with Down syndrome also have problems with speech and language development, communicating with others can be difficult.

Young people and children with Down syndrome may find it hard to express themselves and understand instructions. That can lead to difficulties with taking part in classroom activities.

Learning Social Skills

Children with Down syndrome may face a number of challenges with developing their social skills and joining in with their classmates. It can be difficult for students with the condition to understand subtle social cues and nonverbal communication, such as changing facial expressions and body language. That can make it difficult to join in with group activities in the classroom or socially at break times.

Dealing with Education

While there may be greater challenges in education for young people and children with Down syndrome, they can thrive in school and college just like anyone else. Everyone benefits from inclusive education. That means going to school or college with a diverse range of people, including people with and without disabilities. An inclusive education helps people develop all their skills—academic, social, and personal.

EXTRA HELP AT SCHOOL

Some children who have Down syndrome get extra help in class from teaching assistants. Teaching assistants do not do the student's work for them, but rather help them learn. For example, a child with Down syndrome may find it hard to follow a long list of instructions given for some classwork. In that instance, a teaching assistant can break down the instructions into different sections or find an explanation that the child can understand. They ensure the child has the extra time they need to process instructions or explanations, and help them practice a new piece of knowledge until they feel confident with it.

Teachers and teaching assistants often repeat information until the student remembers it.

LEARNING BY DOING

Many children who have Down syndrome learn best by seeing and doing things themselves, rather than simply being told things. This may be because they find it hard to think about and remember too many things at one time, which makes it difficult for them to learn from a teacher talking to a class for a long time. They often enjoy using a computer because the information on a computer is presented visually on screen, through pictures, sound effects, cartoons, and videos. Seeing and hearing the same information in many different forms helps people with Down syndrome (and many others too) remember it.

HELP FROM TECHNOLOGY

Some learning difficulties are caused by a physical problem, such as trouble holding a pen or paintbrush. In these cases, students with Down syndrome may use assistive devices. Assistive devices are any type of material, equipment, tool, or technology that helps people learn or makes it easier for them to complete tasks.

Students may benefit from using tools that make learning easier, such as special pencils to make writing easier, touchscreen computers, or computers with large-letter keyboards.

Children with Down syndrome learn by watching other students carry out tasks in school. Support from peers also helps students with Down syndrome feel that they belong and creates an accepting and inclusive environment.

Predictable routines at school or college help students with Down syndrome navigate the day.

CHAPTER 2

What Causes Down Syndrome?

Every human being is remarkable and different from anyone else in many ways. However, there are many similarities in the way we are made up, too. Like all other living things, we are made of building blocks called cells. The way each cell develops, grows, and functions depends on the blueprint of instructions found inside it. We call these instructions genes.

What Are Genes?

Genes are made up of a substance called DNA, which is like a genetic code. This code of chemicals acts like an instruction book for the body's cells, just like words in a written manual. Any person's genes contain around 3 billion DNA chemical code units, which contain all the instructions for living that the person needs.

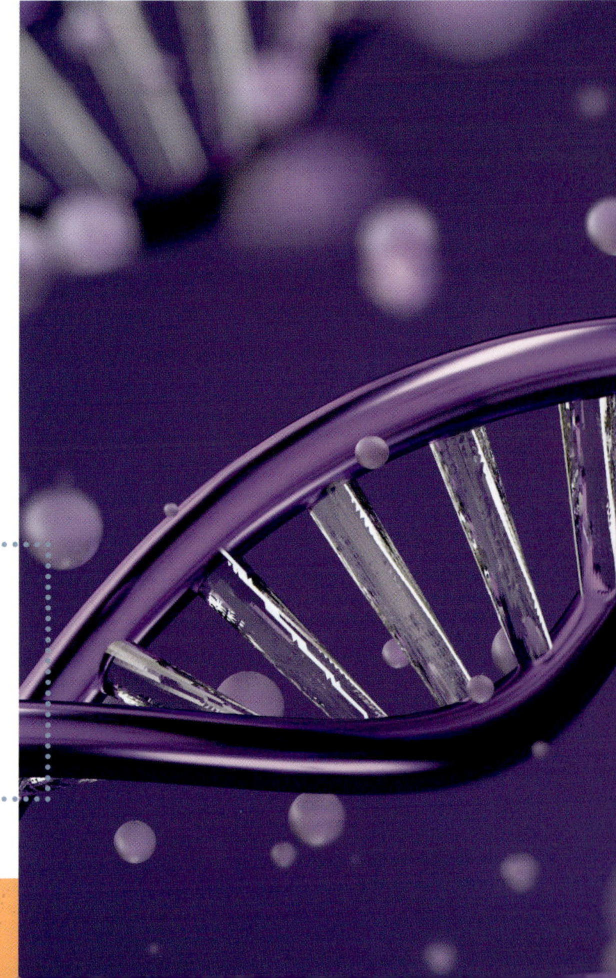

When viewed under powerful microscopes, DNA looks like a ladder twisted into a spiral. Each rung of the ladder is made from varying sequences of four distinct chemicals, like a string of letters completing a word.

Understanding Genes

Genetic instructions in genes determine many different things, such as how a baby's cells develop. Genes control the eye and hair color, and whether a baby is male or female. They instruct parts of cells to make different chemicals. Some are necessary for the cell to function, and others are used by the body to carry out processes, such as helping to digest, or break down, food. Others act as chemical messengers for communicating with other cells and parts of the body.

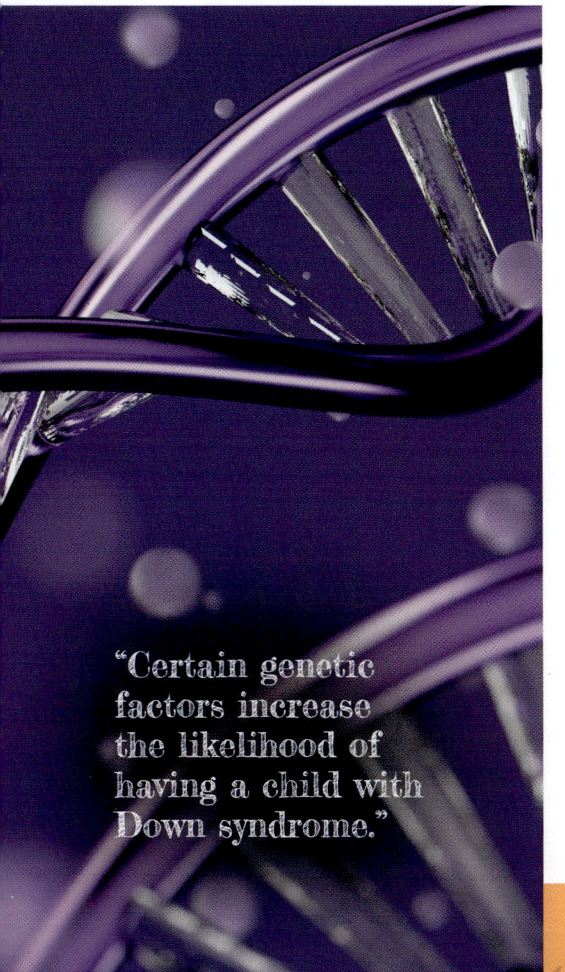

"Certain genetic factors increase the likelihood of having a child with Down syndrome."

When Genes Become Active

Genes for many different things are in place in a cell, but only the ones that are actually turned on and active have any effect. Which ones turn on can be affected by the environment or places and conditions in which a person grows up. For example, someone may have genes that could let them be good at languages or have a great memory for facts. But without the chance to learn, perhaps because of poor schooling or no encouragement to read when that person was young, these genes may remain inactive and such skills may never be discovered.

Chromosomes and Down Syndrome

Genes are packed together and grouped in threadlike structures called chromosomes. These are roughly the shape of an X. They are found in the central part, or nucleus, of cells. Nearly all cells in the human body contain 23 pairs of matching chromosomes, numbered 1 to 23, so there is a set of 46 chromosomes altogether. However, the cells involved in sexual reproduction only contain 23 chromosomes. Down syndrome is a condition that happens because of changes in chromosome numbers that occur after sexual reproduction.

A Problem with Cell Division

Down syndrome is caused by a random error in cell division that results in an extra copy of chromosome 21. Sexual reproduction in humans happens when a sperm cell from the father moves into the ovum (egg) from the mother. This process is called fertilization. Normally, the sperm carries 23 chromosomes, which join with the 23 in the ovum's nucleus, making 46 in total. This means the fertilized egg has a unique combination of chromosomes and genes from each parent. A baby may inherit characteristics, such as hair color, which are controlled by genes from its parents.

How Cell Division Works

Inside a woman, an embryo starts as a single fertilized ovum and grows into a baby that contains thousands of billions of cells at birth, nine months later. The initial cell copies itself by first unzipping the DNA in its 46 chromosomes and copying each chromosome, so there are now 46 pairs. Then it divides in two, with each nucleus containing 23 pairs, for a total of 46 chromosomes. This happens again and again to build up more and more cells. Cells develop into different types to build different body parts.

This embryo is in its early stages, having split into two cells. Cell division repeats and repeats as part of the process of building a baby.

An Extra Copy of a Chromosome

When something happens at random, this means it occurs by chance with no particular reason. The cells of people with Down syndrome contain 47 chromosomes rather than 46. This difference is caused by a random event before, during, or after fertilization, when one cell gets an extra copy of chromosome 21. The extra chromosome and the genes it contains slightly alter the way a person develops. It results in the characteristics of Down syndrome in a baby.

Understanding Down Syndrome

Hundreds of scientists from around the world worked together on the Human Genome Project, a project to identify all human genes and pinpoint their functions. They have identified more than 21,000 genes on the different chromosomes. Around 200 to 300 are found on chromosome 21, the smallest of our chromosomes, containing just 2 percent of the total DNA in cells. One gene on chromosome 21 is called Down syndrome critical region 1, or DSCR1. This gene produces proteins that affect how the nervous system and blood vessels develop. In people with Down syndrome, blood vessels may not develop as well as those in people without the condition.

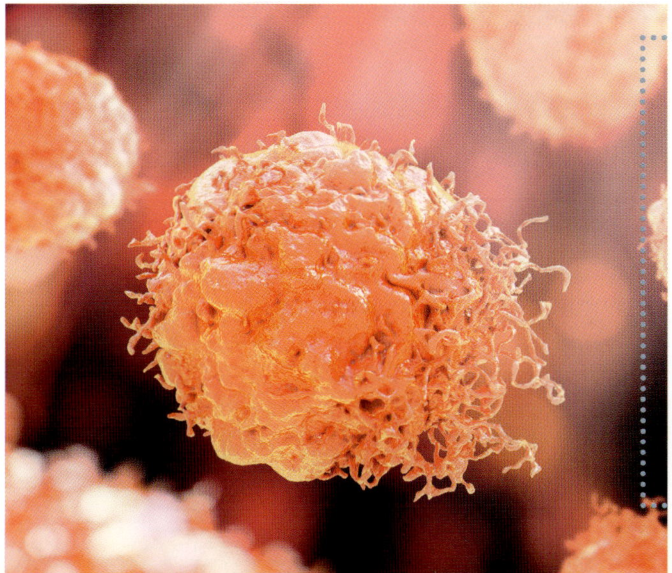

This is an illustration of cancer cells. Studies of people with Down syndrome show that many cancers are less common in them, because tumors cannot grow large without a good blood supply.

Three Types of Changes

Scientists have discovered that there are three distinct types of changes that can lead to Down syndrome. Most people with the condition get their extra chromosome from one parent. This means that one parent's ovum or sperm contains 24 rather than 23 chromosomes, including the extra chromosome 21. This is called complete trisomy 21. Trisomy is a word that blends the Greek word for three (tri) and bodies (soma). It refers to three copies of the same chromosome.

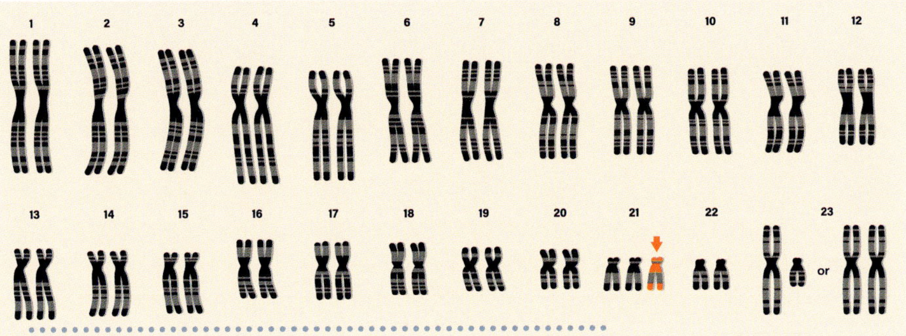

This image shows the extra chromosome 21, which is responsible for Down syndrome.

What Causes a Full Range of Symptoms?

Complete trisomy 21 is the most common cause of Down syndrome. It accounts for 95 percent of cases. The extra chromosome usually randomly occurs in a mother's ovum, but can also happen in a sperm. The extra copy of chromosome 21 is found in all of the cells of the person with the condition. Around 4 percent of people with the syndrome have translocation trisomy 21. In this situation, a small part of an extra copy of chromosome 21 is in their cells. Its chemicals get "stuck" to another chromosome during cell division. People with these two types of trisomy 21 usually experience the full range of symptoms of Down syndrome.

Not Experiencing the Full Range of Symptoms

Mosaic trisomy 21 is when most of someone's cells have 47 chromosomes, but some have 46. This type of trisomy 21 can happen during cell division soon after fertilization between normal ovum and sperm, when one cell produced by cell division gains an extra chromosome from the other cell. When someone has this type of trisomy 21, they do not always have a full range of typical Down syndrome symptoms.

Understanding Down Syndrome

Some diseases and conditions are always inherited. One example is muscular dystrophy, a condition that causes a person's muscles to weaken over the course of their life. If a parent carries a gene for the condition on their chromosomes, they may pass it on to their child. This is not usually the case with Down syndrome, which is generally caused by a change in the number of chromosomes, and genes, in a sperm or ovum. However, in rare cases, parents without Down syndrome may pass it on to their children. In these parents, chemicals making up genes are rearranged between chromosome 21 and neighboring chromosomes. The rearrangement is balanced and it has no effect on the health of the adult. But when passed on, the rearrangement can become unbalanced so the recipient has extra genetic material from chromosome 21, causing translocation trisomy 21. Only about 1 percent of people with Down syndrome inherit their condition in this manner.

By investigating and understanding genes, scientists have been able to pinpoint genetic changes that cause Down syndrome.

Treating Genes

In the future, it may be possible to treat the genes of someone who will grow up with Down syndrome so that they are less affected by its worst aspects. This is possible because scientists have found ways to switch off and even remove inaccurate copies of genes, called mutations, that cause illnesses and replace them with healthy versions. This way of treating the genes of an individual is called gene therapy.

Understanding Gene Therapy

When older people have a damaged hip bone that makes walking painful, surgeons can remove it and replace it with a new metal one that works better. The general principle of gene therapy is similar. Scientists find a section of DNA on a gene that is not functioning properly and might be causing a health problem. They then replace it with a new, functioning gene. The technique of gene editing, or making changes to genes, was first developed in the 1970s. However, it is only in recent times that improved equipment, such as powerful computers and better laboratory techniques for gene editing, have been available for scientists to use. Gene therapy has already been successful in treating some rare inherited illnesses such as severe combined immunodeficiency, in which people have no immunity against bacteria.

Understanding Down Syndrome

Every gene has a job to do in a person, often in combination with other genes. Scientists have so far identified more than 21,000 genes in humans. The total number of genes in the human genome is thought to be around 30,000. Scientists are figuring out the functions of all those genes, and what happens when they do not work properly. For example, some genes may cause cells to make particular proteins to build and repair themselves or to make useful materials in the body, such as digestive juices or blood. When people have an extra chromosome 21 in Down syndrome, gene copies may be interacting, blocking one another's actions, or mutations may be giving wrong instructions to cells on how to develop.

Facing Facts

The Human Genome Project to discover the genes making up all human chromosomes published its first results in 2001. Surprisingly, it found that more than half of our DNA was apparently useless "junk" DNA with no codes to make proteins. Since then, scientists have found that this junk is in fact essential because it regulates when and where genes are turned off and on throughout our bodies.

Genes are responsible for our hair color, the color of our skin, the color of our eyes, and many other features of our bodies.

A Simple Idea

The idea of gene editing is fairly simple. Scientists take a cell from a person with a condition. In a laboratory, they "edit out" the mutated gene and replace it with a normally functioning gene. In the case of Down syndrome, they might remove the mutated form of DSCR1 from a cell and replace it with the equivalent normal version from someone without Down syndrome. But chromosomes are microscopic, and scientists can't simply chop genes out with a scalpel and stick new ones in their place. Instead, they rely on some help from viruses.

Supersmart Viruses

If you have ever had a cold, then you have been attacked by a virus. Viruses are incredibly small living things, much smaller even than bacteria. They have a very simple form consisting of a protein case surrounding a small amount of DNA that holds just a few genes inside. Viruses can survive on their own, sometimes for long periods, but can only reproduce, or make more, once they get inside a living cell. Once inside, they use energy from this host cell to make hundreds of thousands of copies of themselves.

Infecting Cells

Scientists use modified, or altered, viruses as a gene delivery service. They first remove any of the virus's own genes that can cause sicknesses in people, then replace them with the normal, functioning gene to be added in the gene therapy procedure. When this modified virus is placed with human cells in carefully controlled laboratory conditions, the virus gets into the cells. First, specialized proteins on the virus coat attach to certain proteins on the human cell surface. Then, after locking in place, the cells suck the viruses in or the viruses force their way in. The gene they are carrying "infects" the cell with this normal gene, replacing the mutated one.

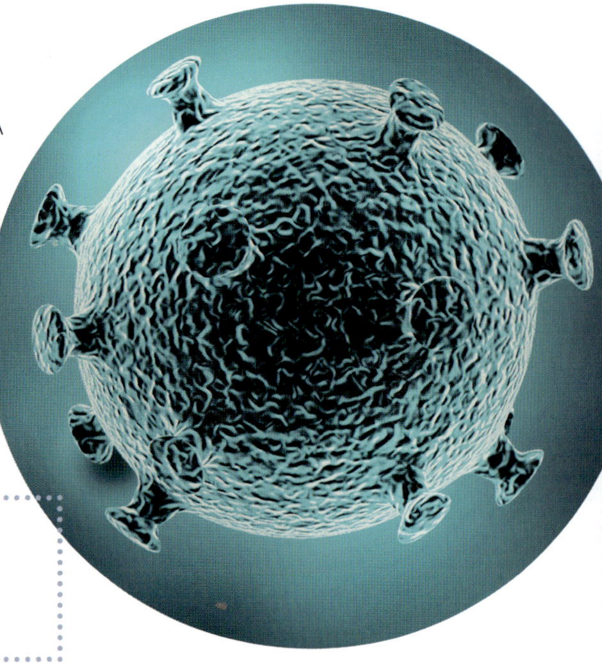

We are usually concerned about viruses, but these often-damaging organisms help humans when we use them for gene therapy.

Understanding Down Syndrome

Not all gene therapies work by replacing a mutation with a normal version of a gene. Some introduce genes that block the way other genes work. Female mammals normally have two copies of X chromosomes in their cells, but only one needs to be active. The reason is that a gene called XIST coats the surface of one of the X chromosomes with a protein blanket that stops its genes from working. Scientists may be able to use XIST in the future to shut down the extra chromosome 21 in people with Down syndrome, which would effectively stop the condition.

Scientific understanding of genetics may become so sophisticated that harmful genes can be "deactivated" before they have a chance to cause damage.

Using Special Cells

Gene therapy does not take place using just any human cell. It happens with special cells called stem cells. Gene therapy that uses stem cells is already available and holds great potential for treating diseases and medical conditions such as Down syndrome.

Understanding How Stem Cells Work

In the human body, there are many distinct and specialized types of cells with different functions. For example, neurons or nerve cells are long and adapted to pass messages through the nervous system. However, skin cells are flat and waterproof, and adapted to hold together and protect the body. Stem cells are not specialized, but instead are shape-shifters, which can develop into any other type of cell. In parts of the body, such as the stomach, bone marrow, skin, and heart, there are supplies of stem cells that can turn into different types of cells to repair, grow, or develop the body. A few days after an ovum is fertilized, stem cells have formed inside the embryo. They then start to change into different specialized types, and different organs and body parts develop.

Making Copies

The other thing about stem cells is that they can make copies of themselves. Specialized cells, such as neurons and blood cells, normally cannot do this, but one stem cell can split over and over to produce millions of cells over many months. And this can be made to happen in glass dishes in laboratories, not just inside a human body.

Scientists speed up the process of splitting stem cells by adding chemicals in a growth solution so stem cells divide quicker. They also add a solution containing the virus for gene editing.

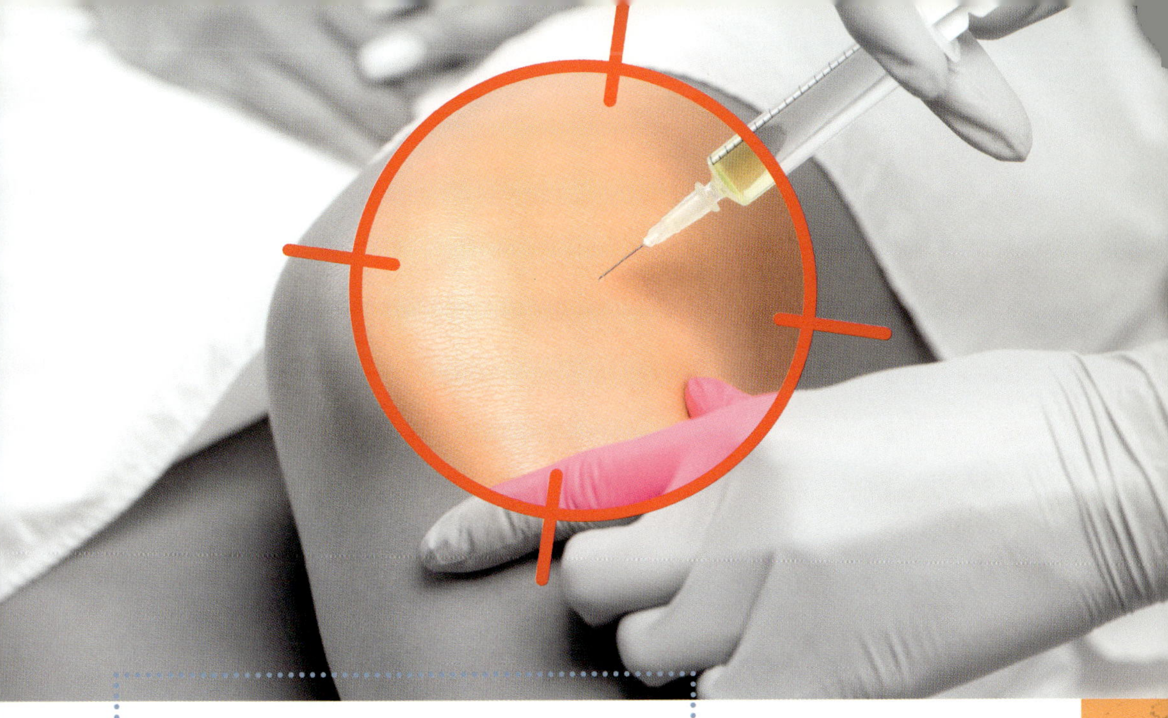

Stem cell therapy is used to treat a number of conditions, such as arthritis, which causes pain and inflammation in the joints.

Into the Body

In stem cell therapy, the solutions are first washed off cells containing the virus. Then the cells are injected with a syringe into a person receiving therapy. Injections are given into veins so the stem cells can spread through the blood, under the skin, into muscles, and sometimes into other body parts, such as the base of the brain.

Understanding Down Syndrome

Once inside a body, stem cells divide further. Scientists believe that the stem cells seek out and repair damaged cells and boost the health of normal cells and, in the process, spread normal copies of the edited gene through a person. For someone born with Down syndrome, such stem cell therapy has the potential to alter the brain's development to possibly reduce or slow mental changes associated with the condition, especially in later life.

Concerns about Gene Therapy

Gene therapy using stem cells has the potential to transform lives. However, such treatment remains controversial. One reason is that such therapies are expensive, meaning that sometimes only people with more money can afford treatment. But a bigger reason for the controversy is the safety of gene therapy.

Testing a New Drug

When a new wonder drug becomes publicly available, it is the result of years of research carried out at universities and companies. There is a long process to find out if any medical discovery is safe and will work. Many therapies are tested first on animals such as mice in laboratories. Then they must be assessed and meet certain standards before receiving approval from countries' regulators for use in treating people. This is how the use of stem cells was approved to help patients' bodies accept transplanted organs, such as hearts, more successfully.

Facing Facts

Stem cell therapies to treat conditions are nearly all new and experimental. Therefore, they may not work, and there may be downsides. For example, stem cells injected into mice in laboratories have been known to divide and produce cancerous growths called teratomas. However, hundreds of companies and organizations worldwide already offer stem cell therapy for a wide range of conditions. In 2017, a company in India claimed to have treated 14 people with Down syndrome. With such publicity, many more people will come forward for similar therapies, with little proof that they will work.

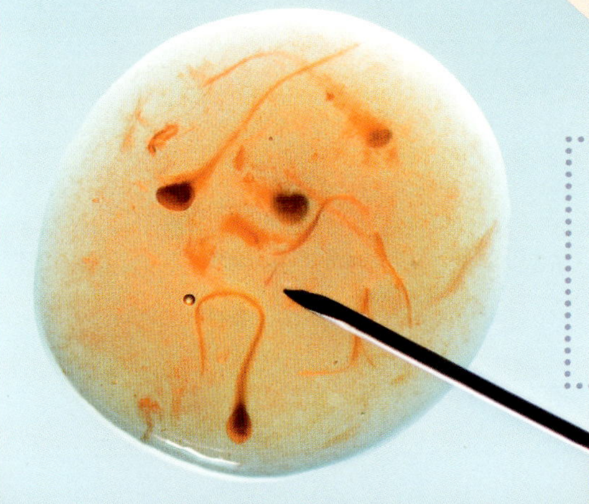

During in-vitro fertilization, sperm is sometimes injected into an egg to fertilize it (see opposite). This process is called intracytoplasmic sperm injection (ICSI).

Finding Stem Cells

Stem cells used for Down syndrome therapy come from embryos. These embryos have not developed inside pregnant women but instead are created during in-vitro fertilization, which is a technique of combining sperm and eggs in laboratories. It is used to help couples have children who cannot conceive naturally. The stem cells come from unused embryos donated for research by the parents. However, some people believe strongly that it is ethically wrong to use cells from any human embryo for therapy.

Problems with the Immune System

A major challenge to gene and stem cell therapy is the body's immune system, which acts like a defensive shield. This system rallies white blood cells to defend other cells in the body when they detect attack by bacteria or viruses. Injected stem cells containing viruses may be recognized as intruders, too. This immune response can tire people and make them sick.

This illustration shows white blood cells attacking a microbe. The immune system is designed to protect the body, but an unusual addition such as a stem cell could cause it to go into overdrive.

Making Life Better

The dream of all gene therapies for different conditions is to make people feel better and be able to live easier, more comfortable lives. For someone with Down syndrome, that could mean an improvement in their ability to coordinate movements or a healthier heart. Such therapies offer the hope of a fix toward a better life, yet might have some hidden costs.

Understanding Down Syndrome

Many people with Down syndrome live happily with their condition. Although they may need more support from care workers and family than some other people would, they can experience lives that are just as rich, fulfilling, and varied as people without Down syndrome. A therapy meant to change a life for the better could cause unexpected problems. For example, changing one gene in a cell might have unexpected effects on cell and organ functions. Repairing the gene DSCR1 might enhance brain function in later life. But, for some individuals, it could increase the likelihood of suffering bouts of depression or bipolar disorder.

Gene therapy is still an experimental treatment that could create future problems as well as treat existing conditions.

Making the Ideal Baby

In the future, doctors may be able to create "designer babies." Genetic testing may one day reveal many potential genes and chromosomal conditions that could affect traits such as IQ, athletic ability, or appearance. Parents may be able to request gene therapies to change the original version of a developing child into one they prefer. There are many pros, such as possibly enhancing a person's life span or quality of life. But there are also many cons, such as the removal of natural variation from societies. Some people are concerned about such interventions, arguing that parents do not have the right to tamper with babies' genes.

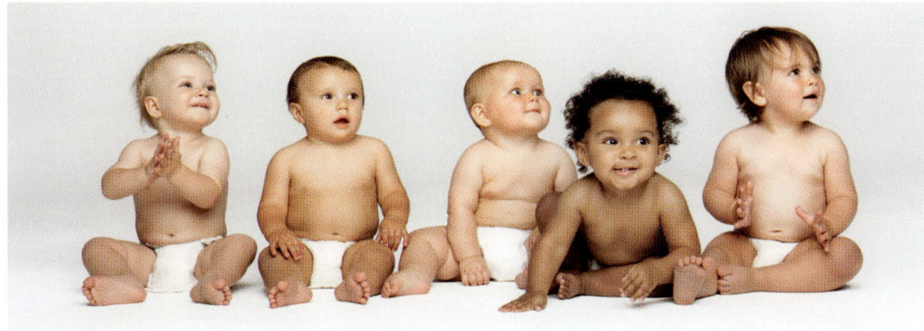

Is it right to turn genes on and off to create an ideal of a perfect baby? Many people do not agree with the idea.

Stem Cell Studies

In 2016, a doctor published a paper claiming remarkable success with stem cell therapy for Down syndrome. Dr Geeta Shroff reported that she had injected stem cells into the muscles and skin of a male baby born with Down syndrome. According to Dr Shroff, the baby showed improvement after three months of treatment. He developed better understanding, better coordination and muscle strength, became more responsive to relatives, started to babble, and his face even changed shape. Many scientists are highly skeptical of these claims. Some say any mental changes that could change coordination, for example, would require the cells to be injected into the brain. They say that this baby was not compared to babies with Down syndrome who were not given similar injections, so many changes were simply the result of normal growth and development.

Social Connections and Down Syndrome

Social connections play an important role in the mental health and wellbeing of everyone, and it's no different for people with Down syndrome. Like all children and young people, some people with Down syndrome may be outgoing and sociable, while others may be shy and find it harder to make friends. They may need a little more support from family and friends, and more chances to practice their social skills.

FORMING RELATIONSHIPS

Children with Down syndrome may have difficulties in developing social skills such as taking turns and sharing, which can make it harder for them to form friendships. They often need help with developing relationship skills over a longer period of time. Difficulties or delays with speech and language can make it more difficult for children with Down syndrome to easily express themselves in social situations. They also often find it harder to play with other children due to difficulties with communicating effectively.

Children with Down syndrome learn to form relationships with family members, just like any other child. But the process can be more complicated for them.

FAMILY PROBLEMS

It can be difficult for both children with Down syndrome and their siblings to navigate relationships. For the child with Down syndrome, expressing their emotions and thoughts can be difficult because of issues with language. That can put a strain on relationships with family members. They may also find it hard to join in with play with brothers and sisters because of problems with understanding social behavior. Siblings may sometimes feel jealous of the attention from parents received by their brother or sister with Down syndrome. They may feel resentful of the life changes that a sibling with a disability brings. Parents will often have to give more attention to a child with a disability, and siblings too may have to help care for them.

Although helping care for a brother or sister with Down syndrome presents challenges, it can be a wonderful experience too.

Facing Stigma

Although today there is more effort than ever in society to create environments that are inclusive and accepting of people with disability, people with Down syndrome still experience stigma and discrimination. Prejudice can make it very difficult for them to join in everyday social events, and may prevent them and their family and friends from doing normal social activities that other people enjoy.

Dealing with Social Connections

For people with Down syndrome, support with forming connections, developing language skills, and learning how to socialize with others is incredibly important. Help with building those skills comes from family, friends, teachers, and other support workers.

THE ROLE OF OCCUPATIONAL THERAPISTS

Occupational therapists help people with physical and learning difficulties develop skills that are needed to form relationships. Therapists work with children on communication, empathy, and problem-solving by using fun activities. For example, an occupational therapist may develop a game aimed at improving concentration or social skills. Occupational therapists often use role-play, observing and copying the social behavior of others, and telling stories that explain social behavior to help people with Down syndrome develop their social skills. The therapists also set up opportunities for children to practice socializing with peers. For example, they may organize activities such as group sports events that teach children how to be part of a group and work as a team.

Family, friends, teachers, and support workers help people with Down syndrome achieve as much as they can for themselves and get the most out of life.

SEEKING SUPPORT

Parents often help their child with Down syndrome develop social skills by inviting other children to their home to play. That helps the child with Down syndrome and other children they may meet at school or in other situations get to know each other. Some children with Down syndrome also like to take part in clubs or groups that focus on learning disabilities similar to their own. They may enjoy meeting and talking with other young people who know how it feels to have Down syndrome. Peer support groups or social clubs specifically for children and young people with Down syndrome provide great opportunities to connect with others of the same age who share similar experiences and interests.

Joining in with community activities such as sports clubs, art classes, and music groups helps people with Down syndrome learn social skills and build friendships in a fun environment.

Teaching that focuses on essential skills such as starting conversations and understanding social cues helps people with Down syndrome learn how to form relationships. Role-playing and practice sessions reinforce these skills.

Encouraging a positive attitude and self-confidence helps people with Down syndrome get the most out of social interactions.

CHAPTER 3

Diagnosing Down Syndrome

After any baby is born, doctors and nurses always thoroughly check the newborn child to confirm that they are healthy and to identify any health conditions. They may start to suspect that a baby has Down syndrome because of aspects of the baby's physical appearance, such as the way their face looks or if the baby weighs significantly less than other babies. These red flags make the health workers look more closely at the child and more carefully examine them for other physical signs of Down syndrome.

Understanding Down Syndrome

One way for healthcare workers to diagnose, or identify, whether a baby has Down syndrome is to perform a careful physical examination of the baby. Signs include decreased or poor muscle tone, which makes the baby seem especially floppy, and a short neck, with excess skin at the back of the neck. Other signs include a slightly flat profile to the face and nose when viewed sideways, upward slanting eyes, and unusually small head, ears, and mouth. On close inspection, there may also be a skin fold that comes out from the upper eyelid and covers the inner corner of the eye. There may also be white spots on the iris, the colored part of the eye, which are called Brushfield spots. There is also often a single deep crease across the palm of the hand, and a deep groove between the first and second toes.

"After birth, a diagnosis of Down syndrome may be suspected if certain physical characteristics are noted."

Babies with Down syndrome often have physical characteristics that indicate the condition is present.

Confirming Diagnosis

Sometimes, some individuals with Down syndrome may not have clear physical signs and symptoms of the condition. On the flip side, many of these symptoms are common in the general population and may not necessarily indicate Down syndrome. For these reasons, hospital workers have to take a sample of the baby's blood to confirm the diagnosis. This type of blood test is called a karyotype. A karyotype test evaluates the chromosomes in a sample of body cells. Results of a karyotype test are usually available about two weeks after the tests has been carried out.

Looking at Cells

Karyotypes allow specialists to identify genetic conditions. First, a blood sample is placed into a special dish or tube and allowed to grow in a laboratory for about two weeks. Later, cells are removed and stained so a specialist can use a microscope to examine the size, shape, and number of chromosomes in the cell sample. The stained sample is photographed to show the arrangement of the chromosomes. This is called a karyotype. In the case of Down syndrome, the cells are examined to see if there is extra material from chromosome 21.

Screening in Pregnancy

With every pregnancy, there is a small chance of having a Down syndrome baby. However, some people are more likely than others to have a child with Down syndrome. Certain tests can detect an increased risk or diagnose Down syndrome during pregnancy.

The Issue of Age

Babies with Down syndrome are born to women of all ages. However, the main thing that increases the chance of having a Down syndrome baby is the mother's age—for example, a woman who is 20 years of age has a 1 in 1,500 chance of having a baby with Down syndrome. This risk factor increases to a 1 in 100 chance when women are 40 years of age, and it becomes 1 in 50 or greater when a woman is 45 years of age or older. The chance of having a child with Down syndrome also increases if someone has previously had a child with Down syndrome. For most people, this chance is still small: around 1 in 100. There's around a 50/50 chance of a child having Down syndrome if one of their parents has the condition.

For younger mothers, the chance of having a baby with Down syndrome is reduced, but still possible.

Blood Tests

A screening test can tell a woman whether her baby has a lower or higher chance of having Down syndrome. Screening tests usually consist of a blood test. In the blood test, the nurse or doctor uses a needle to take a sample of the pregnant woman's blood and checks it for markers, such as certain proteins, that can suggest an increased likelihood that her child might have Down syndrome.

Facing Facts

An ultrasound machine uses sound waves of a very high frequency that produce different echoes when they hit and reflect, or bounce off, different parts inside a human body. Computers can convert the echoes into an image on a monitor. Doctors can use ultrasound to take images inside a pregnant woman's body to see if they can detect fluid at the back of the neck of the fetus, which sometimes indicates Down syndrome. Screening tests such as these do not provide an absolute diagnosis, but they help a pregnant woman decide whether she might like to have a diagnostic test.

Screening tests such as ultrasound scans are safer than diagnostic tests for the mother and the fetus.

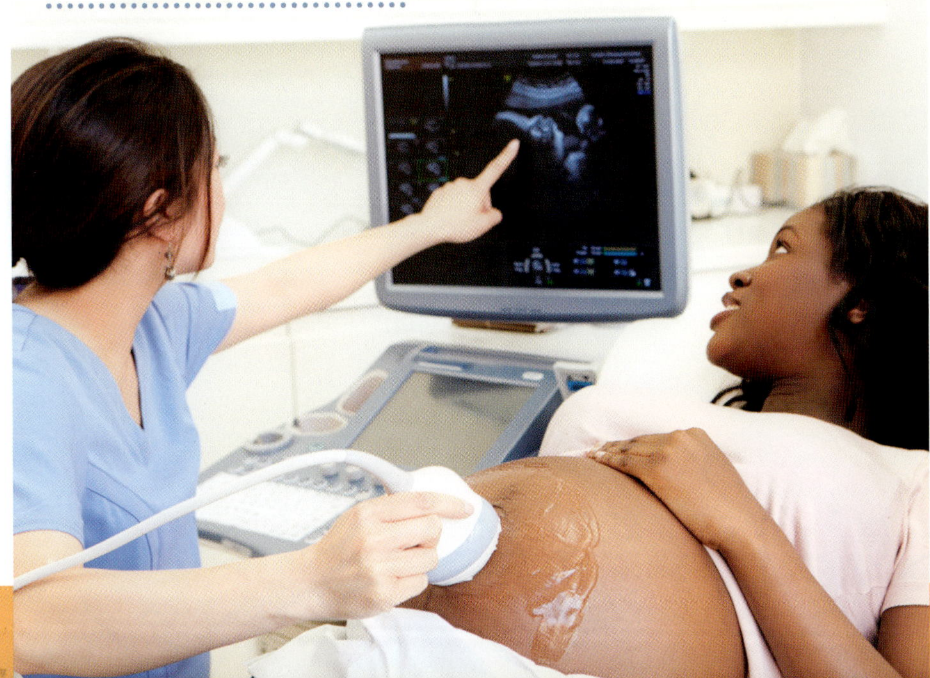

Further Testing

If a screening test suggests an increased likelihood that a fetus has Down syndrome, a diagnostic test can be performed. Diagnostic tests can usually tell whether a baby will have Down syndrome, but they cannot tell parents what impact the condition will have on their individual baby's life.

Collecting a Sample

Diagnostic testing for Down syndrome involves getting and testing a sample of genetic material. To do a diagnostic test, doctors usually insert a long, thin needle through the wall of the abdomen. They use an ultrasound machine to guide them to make sure the needle passes into the sac that surrounds the fetus, then they remove a small sample of fluid from the sac. Getting the sample usually takes about 10 minutes, and is described as uncomfortable rather than painful.

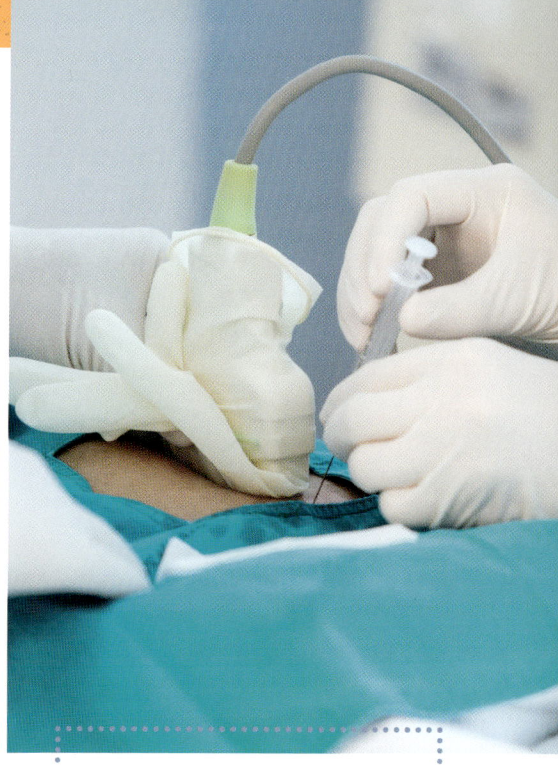

Cells from the fluid extracted from the sac that surrounds a fetus are tested to see if they contain extra material from chromosome 21, which may indicate that a fetus has Down syndrome.

Understanding Down Syndrome

Diagnostic testing for Down syndrome is usually offered to pregnant women who are considered to be at higher risk based on factors such as their age, if they already have a child with Down syndrome, or if there is a family history of the condition. Women are given information about the benefits and risks of diagnostic testing for Down syndrome so they can decide whether to continue with it or not.

Facing Facts

Diagnostic tests involve some risks for the mother and baby. These tests carry a slight risk of miscarriage, or the end of the pregnancy and loss of the baby. The tests can also cause an infection. The other problem is that deciding what to do if the test is positive is very difficult for many people. Parents may see the result as a positive thing, as it means they can continue with the pregnancy while researching information about the condition so they can be fully prepared.

Some parents want to know as much as they can about their baby before it is born, including if there are any issues to be aware of.

CHAPTER 4

Help with Down Syndrome

Many of the medical problems that are common in people with Down syndrome, such as hearing or sight problems, can be treated or corrected. Most children with Down syndrome who have hearing difficulties can be helped by the use of a hearing aid—a device that fits in the ear and makes sounds louder and clearer. Hearing aids are usually offered to children with even just a mild hearing loss to prevent delays in their ability to learn and develop. Glasses can be used to correct nearsightedness or farsightedness, and straightforward operations can solve simple eye problems such as cataracts.

Because of the increased risks of hearing and sight problems, children with Down syndrome should be examined by an eye specialist when they are born and at regular intervals as they grow up.

Improving Speech

Speech and language therapists work with children who have Down syndrome to help them speak more clearly. Therapists may help children by getting them to imitate and repeat sounds, to pronounce letters and words correctly, or to learn and remember words. They may also help children use different ways to communicate while they are learning to speak, such as sign language and pictures.

Keeping Track of Health

Regular health checks and screenings help keep an eye on the overall health of people with Down syndrome. They may include screenings for heart defects, any hearing loss, vision problems, gastrointestinal issues, and other health conditions commonly associated with Down syndrome. Other healthcare providers work with people with Down syndrome and their families to manage any medical conditions or health concerns. This may involve help with medication, diet, and other treatments. People with Down syndrome may have issues with tooth development, gum disease, and oral hygiene. Regular dental checkups and help with keeping on top of oral health are important for preventing dental problems.

Understanding Down Syndrome

Hearing problems make it difficult for people to hear what is going on around them. They can also affect a person's ability to speak because they are unable to listen to other people to learn how words are said properly. Some children who have Down syndrome also have trouble speaking clearly and pronouncing words in a way others can easily understand because the muscles in their mouth and tongue are a little loose or floppy. This makes it harder for them to make certain sounds.

"Regular health checks are important for managing the health of people with Down syndrome."

Treatment for Other Conditions

Children with Down syndrome are usually prone to more medical problems than other children, but many of these problems can be corrected easily with medications or surgery. For example, Down syndrome babies who have a heart defect may be treated with medication, but if the heart problem is more serious, they may have surgery a few days after birth to correct it. Cardiac care specialists work closely with Down syndrome patients and their family or other carers to manage heart conditions, providing ongoing monitoring treatment plans as needed.

Down Syndrome and Epilepsy

Children with Down syndrome are more likely to have epilepsy than children who do not have the condition. Epilepsy is a condition in which people can suddenly suffer seizures. Seizures are a loss of control of the body by the brain. In Down syndrome, epilepsy is most common under the age of two and above the age of 50. People can usually treat seizures with medicines.

People who have Down syndrome may need more ongoing support from family into adulthood to help them manage and monitor health conditions.

Problems with the Thyroid

The thyroid is a gland that makes hormones, which control things such as temperature and energy in the body. In some children with Down syndrome, the thyroid gland makes little or no thyroid hormone. This condition is treated by taking thyroid hormone by mouth throughout one's lifetime.

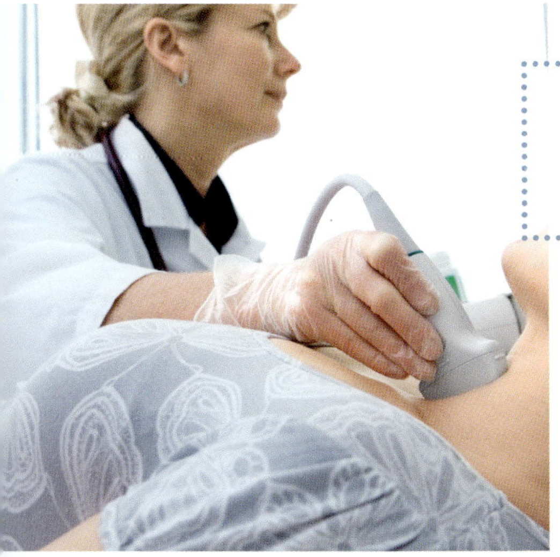

The thyroid gland is sometimes examined by ultrasound scanning if there are concerns it is not functioning properly.

Facing Facts

Children with Down syndrome are between 10 and 30 times more likely than other children to develop leukemia—a cancer of the white blood cells. Children who get leukemia get cancer treatment in the hospital, and many recover completely. Other blood disorders such as anemia (low iron in the blood) may get better by themselves or they can be treated by taking medications.

Understanding Down Syndrome

To determine why children with Down syndrome are more prone to leukemia, scientists studied mice that had an extra copy of 31 genes found on chromosome 21 in humans. Leukemia happens when the body produces too many immature B cells—a type of white blood cell that normally fights infections. Testing mouse cells, scientists found that this happened because a group of proteins called PRC2 were not working. By switching off each of the 31 genes in the mouse cells one by one, scientists discovered that when gene HMGN1 was turned off, the cells stopped growing and died. This proved that the extra copy of gene HMGN1 in people with Down syndrome is important for turning off PRC2 and causing leukemia.

Keeping Healthy

People who have Down syndrome need to do much the same things as everyone else to keep fit and healthy, such as eating a range of healthy foods, getting regular exercise, and taking care of their bodies. Everyone needs to eat a healthy diet that includes protein and fat every day, plenty of fruit and vegetables, and carbohydrates such as pasta, potatoes, and rice. People also need to drink plenty of water every day to keep their bodies functioning properly.

Looking at Food

Most people with Down syndrome eat a normal diet, although those who have digestive problems may have to eat a carefully controlled diet their entire lives. For example, around 6 percent of people with Down syndrome have celiac disease—a condition in which the body cannot properly digest malt, barley, rye, and wheat products. To prevent problems, people have to avoid eating any of these foods. Down syndrome may also increase the risk of gum disease, so individuals should look after their teeth and visit the dentist for regular checkups.

Using Exercise

Like other people, those with Down syndrome benefit from regular physical activity, such as walking or playing sports. Some children with Down syndrome also see a physical therapist when they are young. Physical therapists do activities and exercises with them that help increase the strength of their muscles and improve the way they move. Physical therapy can help very young children with Down syndrome to turn over, crawl, and reach. These skills, in turn, help them do other things and to learn about the world around them.

Exercise is an important part of life for people with Down syndrome. Learning to move properly at a young age also prevents health problems that might otherwise develop later on. For example, if a physical therapist helps a young child walk properly, this stops them from walking in a way that might lead to foot pain or other issues.

Understanding Down Syndrome

Most children receive vaccinations or immunizations while they are young. Vaccinations are injections of a very small, safe amount of weakened or killed viruses or bacteria. The body's immune system learns to recognize and attack the virus or bacteria. If a person gets a real infection later in life, their system knows what to do and can stop them from becoming sick. Down syndrome often causes immune system problems that make it difficult for the body to fight off infections. That is why it is very important for children with Down syndrome to receive all available immunizations.

Mental Health and Down Syndrome

People with Down syndrome are at greater risk of having mental health conditions, including anxiety and depression. There is also the added complication that communication difficulties associated with Down syndrome, such as speech delays and problems with language, can make it difficult for people with the condition to express their emotions. Rather than talking about how they are feeling, they may instead become agitated or angry, or withdrawn. That, in turn, can make it very difficult for people who care for them to identify issues with depression and anxiety.

DEALING WITH CHANGE

People with Down syndrome may be more sensitive to their environment than other people. Changes in their surroundings or routines can be difficult for them to manage, and can trigger feelings of anxiety. Before a big event or a big change, the anxiety may show in physical symptoms such as headaches, stomachaches, tiredness, or changes in appetite and sleep patterns. They may also show in emotional outbursts such as tearfulness or extreme agitation. Other people may become disconnected from what is going on around them and appear emotionally numb and disinterested in things.

A CHANGE IN BEHAVIOR

Because people with Down syndrome struggle to express feelings through words, they are more likely to show signs of distress through behavior. They may start to regress, or go backward, with skills such as using the toilet or social skills. They may eat more or eat less, as their emotional health has an effect on their appetite and eating patterns. Self-harming is also more likely, and includes behavior such as biting, scratching, or hitting oneself.

Other Conditions and Down Syndrome

Some people with Down syndrome experience chronic headaches, back pain, and joint pain. Down syndrome can also suppress the immune system, which makes people more likely to get infections and illnesses. Chronic stress is often associated with Down syndrome, and that can lead to recurring infections, problems with healing wounds, and a greater chance of developing complicated autoimmune disorders.

When struggling with anxiety or depression, people with Down syndrome may show less interest in activities that they previously enjoyed and spend more time alone.

Headphones can help block out loud noises that people with Down syndrome may find difficult to deal with and find very stressful.

Dealing with Mental Health

Because it can be difficult for people with Down syndrome to express themselves, it is important that family, friends, and healthcare professionals look out for signs of distress. By understanding what those signs may be and reacting quickly if they are spotted, people with Down syndrome can be supported and helped through difficulties.

HELP WITH SHOWING FEELINGS

Speech and language can be difficult for people with Down syndrome, so using different types of communication helps explore issues that may be troubling them. For example, pictures of faces showing different emotions can be useful—often, holding up a sad face is an easier way to express unhappiness than speaking the words, "I'm sad." Because people with Down syndrome may not be able to express themselves verbally, specially trained therapists help patients work through emotions. However, it can be difficult for people to find therapists who are trained in understanding the condition and working with Down syndrome patients.

Using images to express emotions can be a much easier way for a person with Down syndrome to show what they are feeling than expressing it verbally.

A HEALTHY ENVIRONMENT

Very busy, chaotic, and stressful environments are often not good for people with Down syndrome struggling with their mental health. Supportive and calm places that do not have too many triggering stimuli, such as bright lights and loud noises, can help people with Down syndrome and ADHD or autism feel less stressed. Quiet spaces, calming activities, and predictable routines all help reduce stress and anxiety.

SUPPORT FROM SOCIETY

Stigma, misconceptions, and negative attitudes toward disabilities such as Down syndrome can be very difficult to deal with, both for those with the condition and their family and friends. A more inclusive and welcoming attitude from people makes it much easier for people with Down syndrome to socialize and that improves their mental wellbeing.

Consistent daily routines can reduce anxiety in people with Down syndrome and help them feel more in control of what is happening around them.

Creative activities such as painting, music, and drama all help people with Down syndrome find healthy nonverbal ways to express themselves, which is good for their mental wellbeing.

CHAPTER 5

Living with Down Syndrome

The life expectancy for people with Down syndrome has increased from 25 years old in 1983 to 60 years old today, with some who have Down syndrome living to more than 80 years old. After school, some young adults with Down syndrome go on to college or leave home and live fairly independently. Others find jobs and roles in their community, but continue to live at home.

Finding a Home

Some young adults with Down syndrome continue to live with their families after they finish high school because they want to or need to. Others want greater independence as they move into adulthood. They may choose to live in a home of their own, with or without roommates, with the help of support services if and when they are needed. Some share a home with other individuals with disabilities and have 24-hour, 7-days-a-week support staff to help them manage.

"While there may be challenges associated with Down syndrome, people with this condition also possess great strengths, abilities, and qualities that enrich the lives of those around them."

Starting a Family

Some people assume that people with Down syndrome and learning difficulties cannot get married, but this is not the case. Some couples get married and live independently, sometimes with family living next door to help out when needed. If couples with Down syndrome get married, they may not have children. This is partly because many cannot have children. If a woman with Down syndrome does have a child, there is a 35 to 50 percent chance of the child having Down syndrome trisomy 21 or other developmental disabilities, so couples may choose not to start a family due to the risk of having a child with the condition too.

Teenagers and young adults with Down syndrome often want to date or think about marriage.

Facing Facts

As they get older, not everyone with Down syndrome develops dementia, but they are at increased risk of doing so. Dementia is a condition that causes memory loss and forgetfulness. Up to 70 to 80 percent of people with Down syndrome over the age of 60 may develop dementia. Dementia tends to occur at an earlier age in people with Down syndrome compared to the general population. Symptoms may start to appear when people are in their 40s or even earlier, which is unusually young compared with the rest of the general population. Scientists think that the increased risk of dementia, like other health issues associated with Down syndrome, results from the extra genes present in people with the condition.

A Plan for Dealing with Down Syndrome

There are many daily hurdles that people with Down syndrome have to overcome. However, living with the condition can be made more manageable by using certain strategies and getting the right support. Planning for healthcare needs, education, housing, employment, and ongoing support with all of those areas can make it easier for people to live with greater independence.

Strategies That Help

For people with Down syndrome who want to live independently from their families, finding the right type of housing is important. That might be living in an assisted facility, where there is help for people if they need it. For example, it might be a group-living situation, in which a group of people with Down syndrome live together in shared accommodation, usually with the support of caregivers.

Assisted living: This type of accommodation provides people with Down syndrome with a safe environment, connections with others who share the same experiences as them, and support with day-to-day living as needed. Group living usually provides easy access for people with Down syndrome to healthcare services, therapy, and education programs. Sometimes, people with Down syndrome choose to live part of the time in assisted living accommodation and part of the time at home with their family.

Managing ongoing health conditions: Keeping healthy can also be challenging for adults with Down syndrome. Dealing with medical appointments, medication, and other forms of treatment if they are needed can be time-consuming and complex. Long-term support with monitoring and managing health often needs to be part of the support system put in place once a person leaves home.

With help from family and support workers, it is far easier for people with Down syndrome to live independent lives today.

Further education and work: Going to college and getting a job are today far more achievable than they once were for people with Down syndrome. Colleges now have programs in place to help people with the condition study and get the most out of their experience. Likewise, employers are becoming much more inclusive of people with disability and encourage more diversity in the workplace, so options for getting a job are much better.

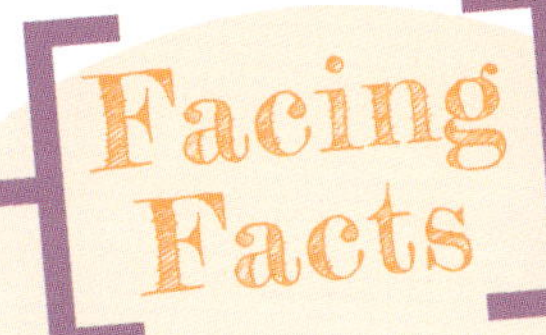

Certain issues make it more difficult for people with Down syndrome to live independently than others. That can include problems with memory and organization, which can make managing a home independently challenging. Help with managing finances may be needed, such as budgeting, paying bills, and dealing with financial systems.

Colleges now have programs in place to help people with Down syndrome study with flexibility and get the most out of their college experience.

Employment and Down Syndrome

People with Down syndrome often come across many challenges and barriers when looking for a job, despite having a strong desire to work. Many of these barriers come from misconceptions about the condition, such as a belief that people with Down syndrome cannot work. Other barriers come from a lack of adaptation in the workplace to make it more suitable for people with disabilities.

OBSTACLES IN THE WAY

People with Down syndrome may find it difficult to get the skills and work experience necessary to apply for and do certain jobs. Because people with Down syndrome often have problems with speech and language, that can make it difficult for them to express thoughts and understand and follow spoken or written instructions. Employers may believe these issues will lessen performance in the workplace, and avoid employing people with Down syndrome as a result.

Some employers have welcomed people with Down syndrome into their organizations, but many are still unaware of the contributions and value that people with the condition can bring to the workforce.

WORKPLACES THAT WORK FOR EVERYONE

People with Down syndrome may need their workplace to be adapted to help them to perform job tasks effectively. They may require modified workstations as well as assistive technology and more flexible schedules. Transportation to work is not always easy for people with the condition too, and that can hold them back from finding employment that suits them.

Still a Stigma

Negative attitudes about intellectual disabilities, including Down syndrome, have led to stigma and discrimination in the workplace. Employers may have misconceptions about the abilities of people with Down syndrome and be reluctant to hire them. Unfortunately, there can also be discrimination from coworkers when people with the condition are hired.

More and more people with Down syndrome are going to work, but there are still many who find it difficult to get employment.

Dealing with Employment

Thankfully, employers are increasingly recognizing that people with Down syndrome have valuable skills, talents, and contributions to offer in the workplace. By breaking down the barriers in the way of getting a job, such as helping with transportation and extra training where needed, they are making workplaces more accommodating. Today, going to work has become a more realistic option for people with disabilities.

Some people with Down syndrome find a job by applying for and competing for one like anybody else, and they work independently without any extra support.

A LOT TO GIVE

The skills and positive contribution that people with Down syndrome make to a workplace are many, including:

- A dedication to the job and a strong work ethic
- A positive attitude and enthusiasm, which rubs off on other employees too
- An attention to detail and focus on completing tasks
- An ability to work as part of a team and inspire others to do so
- A friendly manner that makes for great customer service

MAKING A MATCH

There are now job-matching services that connect people with Down syndrome to job opportunities that match their skills, interests, and abilities. Vocational training programs and workshops that develop skills specifically for the workplace also help those with Down syndrome get the important skills and work experience needed to land a job.

RESPECT AND SUPPORT

Employers are becoming more educated about the benefits of hiring individuals with disabilities, including Down syndrome. By understanding the value of diverse, inclusive workplaces, organizations are now more open to welcoming people with disability into the workforce.

Making accommodations to the workplace helps people with Down syndrome get into work and do their jobs well.

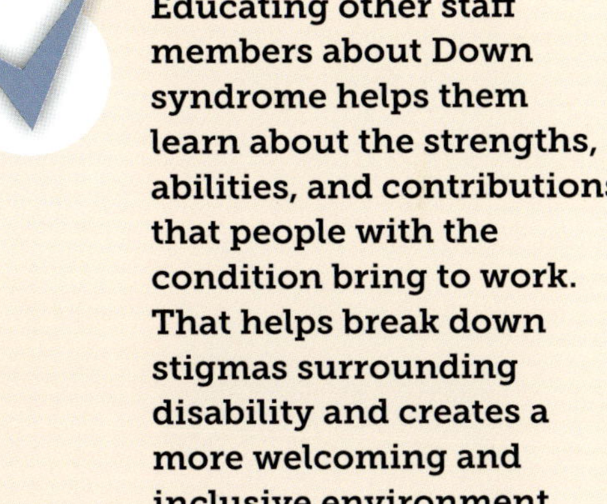

Educating other staff members about Down syndrome helps them learn about the strengths, abilities, and contributions that people with the condition bring to work. That helps break down stigmas surrounding disability and creates a more welcoming and inclusive environment.

CONCLUSION

Down Syndrome and the Future

The future is more hopeful than ever for many people with Down syndrome. Life expectancy has increased as a result of better medical care and understanding of the social and physical needs of people with Down syndrome. Also, research on Down syndrome is making great advances in identifying the genes in chromosome 21 that cause the syndrome. In the future, it may be possible for scientists to improve, correct, or prevent many of the problems associated with Down syndrome.

Living Full Lives

People with Down syndrome now live fuller, richer lives than ever, by attending mainstream schools, contributing to their communities, and having relationships, for example. Now that people with Down syndrome are living longer, the needs of adults with Down syndrome are receiving greater attention.

With assistance from family and care workers, many adults with Down syndrome have developed the skills required to hold down jobs and live independently into later life.

Understanding Down Syndrome

Some people with Down syndrome still face prejudice and exclusion. One way to reduce this is with improved education about the condition. Another is a raised public profile of people with the condition, such as actors with Down syndrome on mainstream television shows.

"Increased spending by governments and better training programs will help more adults with Down syndrome remain healthy and safe, especially when living independently."

Further Findings

Research on Down syndrome has the potential to improve the clinical care and quality of life for individuals with Down syndrome and their families. Scientists are constantly finding out new things about chromosomes, as well as new treatments for people with Down syndrome. Recent findings and new technology are helping. They include:

- A short section at the end of chromosome 21 may be a sign that someone with Down syndrome will develop early dementia.
- Giving pregnant women supplements of choline, a nutrient similar to vitamin B, has lasting effects on the learning, understanding, and spatial awareness of their babies. This could be especially useful for babies with Down syndrome.
- Portable electronic devices that monitor physical activity can help keep track of the physical activity that is so important for people with Down syndrome.

accommodating willing to make adjustments in order to meet the needs of others

adapted changed something to improve it

agitation on edge and irritable

anxiety a state of fear or worry

assembling putting together

asthma a respiratory condition characterized by inflammation and narrowing of the airways, leading to symptoms such as wheezing, shortness of breath, coughing, and chest tightness

bacteria tiny organisms that can cause infections or diseases

benefits positive effects

bipolar disorder a mental health condition characterized by periods of extreme happiness followed by periods of depression

body language nonverbal communication

bone marrow the soft, spongy tissue found within bones

cancerous describing harmful cells, tissues, or growths that have the potential to spread to other parts of the body

chromosomal related to threadlike structures found in cells that carry genetic information

chromosomes threadlike structures found in cells that carry genetic information

cognitive relating to thought, memory, or understanding

contributions acts or things given that benefit others

controversial causing disagreements and conflicting viewpoints

coordinate to synchronize movements, mainly of the legs and arms

dedication commitment to doing something

depression feelings of sadness and hopelessness

disabilities physical or mental impairments that limit normal activities

discrimination unfair treatment or prejudice toward a person or a group of people based on certain characteristics, such as race, gender, age, disability, or religion

diverse including a variety of people with different abilities, gender, beliefs, backgrounds, cultures, races, and experiences

donated given

embryo the early stage of development after fertilization of an egg cell by a sperm cell but before the organism becomes a fetus

empathy the ability to understand and share the feelings, thoughts, and experiences of others

enhancing making better

enthusiasm eagerness, passion, or excitement for something

epilepsy a neurological disorder that causes seizures due to abnormal electrical activity in the brain

ethically in keeping with values

facial expressions nonverbal communication shown through movements and changes in the face, including expressions of emotions such as happiness, sadness, surprise, and fear

fetus a growing, unborn baby

host cell a cell that provides a suitable environment for the survival of another organism

immature not fully developed

immunity the body's ability to defend itself against infection

impact having an effect on something in a significant way

inclusive encouraging the inclusion of diverse groups of people

inherit to receive genetic traits, characteristics, or conditions from biological parents

interacting communicating with others

IQ a measure of intelligence based on certain tests

isolation feeling separated from others

life expectancy the length of time an organism is expected to live

mammals animals that give birth to live young and feed them with milk from their bodies

microscopic too small to be seen without the aid of a microscope

misconceptions views and beliefs based on facts that may not be true

monitor to check the progression of something

motivate to encourage

mutations permanent changes in the DNA sequence of a gene

nervous system the complex network of nerves, cells, and tissues that controls and coordinates senses, movement, and other functions in the body

organ a body part such as the heart or the brain

peers individuals of similar age, often belonging to the same social group or community

prejudice attitudes toward individuals or groups based on unfounded beliefs, often leading to unfair treatment

regulating controlling

resentful a feeling of bitterness

retain to keep hold of

scalpel a sharp knife used to perform surgery

skeptical having doubts about something

sociable wanting to spend time with other people

social cues nonverbal signs given by other people in social situations, such as facial expressions and body movements

stigma a negative attitude, belief, or perception toward a person based on their characteristics

stimuli things that trigger the senses of sight, touch, taste, smell, and hearing

stockier shorter and more thickset

subtle delicate and not easily spotted

transplanted surgically transferred from one location to another

tumors collections of cells that make up growths in the body that can be dangerous

verbal expressed through words

viruses tiny infectious organisms that can replicate, or copy themselves, inside other organisms and cause disease

vocational related to work or a job

work ethic the desire to work

Find Out More

Books

Goldstein, Ellie. *Against All Odds: My Life with Down Syndrome*. SPCK Publishing, 2023.

Hirschmann, Kris. *Kids and Autism* (Diseases and Disorders of Youth). ReferencePoint Press, 2018.

Schwartz, Heather E. *Genetics Breakthroughs* (Edge of Medicine). Mayo Clinic Press Kids, 2023.

Websites

Find out more about Down syndrome at:
https://kidshealth.org/en/kids/down-syndrome.html

Learn more about Down syndrome at:
www.cdc.gov/ncbddd/birthdefects/downsyndrome.html

Truth or myth? Discover some common misconceptions about Down syndrome at:
www.globaldownsyndrome.org/about-down-syndrome/misconceptions-vs-reality

Publisher's note to educators and parents:
All the websites featured above have been carefully reviewed to ensure that they are suitable for students. However, many websites change often, and we cannot guarantee that a site's future contents will continue to meet our high standards of educational value. Please be advised that students should be closely monitored whenever they access the Internet.

Index

About the Author

Sarah Eason has written many books for children and young adults. Researching and writing this book has highlighted the complexities of Down syndrome, from its causes to management, and the challenges that people with the condition face. She hopes this book is an informative, helpful, and compassionate resource for readers interested in the topic or affected by it.